HOW TO SURVIVE RETIREMENT

A Hilarious Guide for the Recently Retired

ILLUSTRATED BY
IAN BAKER

KATE FREEMAN

summersdale

HOW TO SURVIVE RETIREMENT

Text by Colin "Cee Tee" Jackson

Illustrations by Ian Baker

An Hachette UK Company
www.hachette.co.uk

Summersdale Publishers
Part of Octopus Publishing Group Limited
Carmelite House
50 Victoria Embankment
LONDON
EC4Y 0DZ
UK

www.summersdale.com

This FSC® label means that materials and other controlled sources used for the product have been responsibly sourced

FSC www.fsc.org MIX Paper | Supporting responsible forestry FSC® C016973

The authorized representative in the EEA is Hachette Ireland, 8 Castlecourt Centre, Dublin 15, D15 XTP3, Ireland (email: info@hbgi.ie)

Printed and bound in China

ISBN: 978-1-83799-511-0
eISBN: 978-1-83799-512-7

INTRODUCTION

Congratulations! You've made it – you're retired!

No more tortuous commutes, no more tedious meetings and no more need to be civil to colleagues you dislike. A new life of fun and relaxation awaits.

Retirement, though, is not without its own challenges. How will you fill your day? How should you deal with those excruciatingly boring family commitments? Relatives and friends may seek to exploit your congenial good nature and hard-earned free time. Unless you're careful, the burden of fresh expectation will be thrust upon you.

Whatever concerns you may have, this book will show you how to survive retirement.

For an easy life,
show a complete ineptitude
for DIY at all times.

WET PAINT
DAYTIME TV

Avoid at all costs the
mind-numbing, sleep-inducing
tedium of daytime television.

Enjoy an undisturbed sleep by clearing all obstructions and memorizing the steps from your bed to your bathroom.

Immerse yourself in sport
to maintain a healthy,
active lifestyle.

REGULAR AFTERNOON NAPS ARE FURTHER ENHANCED BY UTILIZING THE NEW, LUXURIOUS RECLINING SEATS AT YOUR LOCAL CINEMA.

Z Z Z Z
Z Z Z

TIKI KITCHEN

Reorganize your kitchen to suit your new relaxation-based lifestyle.

CAR MILEAGE, HOUSEHOLD EXPENSES, THE FREQUENCY OF VOWELS IN A WORDLE PUZZLE – SPREADSHEETS ARE THE FUTURE!

SPREADSHEET

Impress your neighbours by spending some of your pension on external home and garden improvements.

You are entitled, expected and *allowed* to be "grumpy". Don't let the side down!

Retirement means you can attend music festivals, as in your youth – though perhaps with a few more home comforts.

Take your new pride and joy out for a spin and show it off to friends.

ALLOTMENTS

Rather than watching the clock at work, spend quality time watching nature's clock.

FAMILY FINANCES ARE IMPORTANT, OF COURSE. PERHAPS, THOUGH, YOU SHOULD CONSIDER ANOTHER MEANS OF DISCUSSING THEM.

PENSIONS VS BILLS

Coffee
SHOP

Try not to look too smug
or self-satisfied when
around non-retirees.

BEING RETIRED MEANS NO LONGER CARING ABOUT FAD DIETS AND TRENDS. ACCEPT THAT YOU'RE "BEACH BODY READY" AS YOU ARE!

JAZZ
BIG BAND
ROCK
GARAGE

Use your new-found time to complete those essential tasks you've been putting off.

With so much free time, don't be surprised if craft fairs and farm shops become places of special interest.

COUNTY
CRAFT
FAIR

With all the experience
and knowledge you've
gathered over the years,
why not write a book?

You don't have to be a social media "influencer" to benefit from free stuff and cut-price deals.

BUS
PASS
BUS
PASS

Being home all day, you'll discover why your cat was always asleep when you came in from work.

BEING HOME ALL DAY, YOU'LL ALSO DISCOVER HOW MANY ROAD TRAFFIC ACCIDENTS YOU'VE APPARENTLY BEEN INVOLVED IN.

Music soothes the soul, so they say. Learn to play a musical instrument.

IF YOU LIVE WITH A PARTNER, RETIREMENT IS THE PERFECT OPPORTUNITY TO START SPENDING MORE QUALITY TIME WITH THEM.

THE
RETIREMENT
CHANNEL

With more time at home, you can finally discover the purpose of all those mysterious buttons on your TV remote.

Time is no longer of the essence.

BISTRO

BEEP BEEP
BEEP
BEEP BEEP

Now there's no need
to rush, you can happily
appreciate the beauty of
your wonderful countryside.

Become an expert on a topic that interests you – and don't be shy about sharing that knowledge with friends.

WINE
WINE
WINE

Now you're retired,
don't allow your
fitness levels to drop.
Realize the importance
of stretching.

YOUR IDEA OF WHAT CONSTITUTES A "GOOD NIGHT OUT" MAY CHANGE WITH TIME.

THINGS TO DO
VISIT FRANCE
HOLIDAYS IN THE USA

Stay organized with a to-do list. Be sure to include all the wonderful and exciting things you now have time to enjoy.

ENROL IN DAYTIME CLASSES TO DEVELOP THAT TALENT YOU ALWAYS KNEW YOU HAD.

Z
Z
Z
Z

With no early morning starts for work, you can party all hours of the... afternoon!

You didn't quite grasp the extent of climate change, travelling to and from a comfortable office job, did you?

Home made
Lemonade

Bored? Missing the excitement of your old work environment? Why not start up your own small, part-time business?

Avoid doing anything that could result in you being called to an urgent and top-level "meeting".

Enjoy not being at work and having to attend the dreaded daily morning huddle. Have a morning cuddle instead.

DON'T BE TOO QUICK VOLUNTEERING TO LOOK AFTER YOUR GRANDCHILDREN.

DEPARTURES

TICKETS

Relieve the dreadful
stress of regular holidays,
day trips and social events
by making your childhood
dream come true.

SAVE THE MONEY PREVIOUSLY DONATED TO STAFF WHIP-ROUNDS BY TREATING YOURSELF WHENEVER YOU GET THE CHANCE.

BISTRO

Now you're no longer working, there's no need to send all those Christmas cards to colleagues anymore.

Leave the house whenever possible, in case your address becomes the drop-off point for your working neighbours' mail orders.

SANDWICH SHOP
THE WHITE SWAN PUB

Support local businesses – money previously spent on sandwiches can now be spent on lunch in the neighbouring pub.

Maybe don't tell ex-colleagues the enjoyment you get from listening to traffic reports on the local radio.

BUS
TRAIN

It's probably best not to label your food in the kitchen cupboard as you did in the staff canteen.

DON'T WASTE YOUR WELL-EARNED TIME. MAKE THE MOST OF EACH DAY AND ENJOY YOUR RETIREMENT!

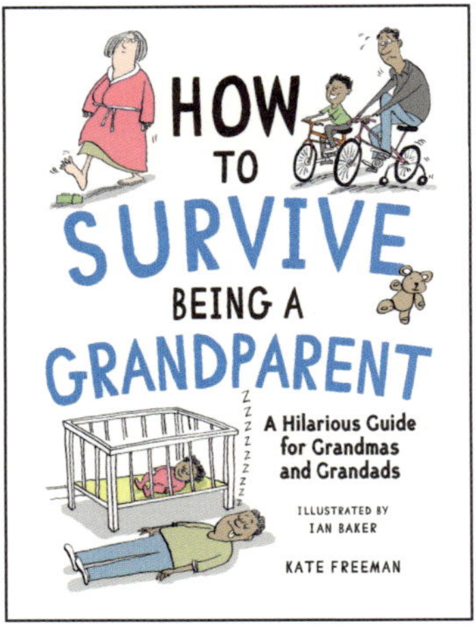

HOW TO SURVIVE BEING A GRANDPARENT

ISBN: 978-1-83799-513-4 · Hardback

ATTENTION ALL GRANDPARENTS!

This book is the essential guide to navigating the treacherous waters of spoiling grandchildren, mastering the art of babysitting, perfecting your cake-baking skills and much more. Charmingly illustrated, this tongue-in-cheek guide will have you chuckling from page to page.

THE LITTLE INSTRUCTION BOOK FOR SENIORS

ISBN: 978-1-83799-371-0 · Hardback

It really is the life in your years that counts

Now that you're a senior, you'll come to realize that there is nothing that can't be fixed by a quick trip to the garden centre, that your "bad back" will reliably get you out of any tricky situation and that it's now socially acceptable to call anyone younger than you "Dear" rather than remember their actual name. In other words, now the real fun begins!

Encouraging you to laugh, embrace life and enjoy the ride, the pearls of wisdom in this no-nonsense handbook will guide you through all the pleasures and pitfalls of your senior years.

Have you enjoyed this book?
If so, find us on Facebook at
Summersdale Publishers, on Twitter/X
at **@Summersdale** and on Instagram
and TikTok at **@summersdalebooks**
and get in touch.

We'd love to hear from you!

www.summersdale.com